One...Two...Three...
SASSAFRAS!

by Stuart J. Murphy · illustrated by John Wallace

HarperCollinsPublishers

LEVEL
1

To Madeleine Grace—with her smiley face!
—S.J.M.

To Zach, Jake, and A.J.
—J.W.

The publisher and author would like to thank teachers Patricia Chase, Phyllis Goldman, and Patrick Hopfensperger for their help in making the math in MathStart just right for kids.

HarperCollins®, ◼®, and MathStart® are registered trademarks of HarperCollins Publishers. For more information about the MathStart series, write to HarperCollins Children's Books, 1350 Avenue of the Americas, New York, NY 10019, or visit our website at www.mathstartbooks.com.

Bugs incorporated in the MathStart series design were painted by Jon Buller.

One . . . Two . . . Three . . . Sassafras!
Text copyright © 2002 by Stuart J. Murphy
Illustrations copyright © 2002 by John Wallace

Library of Congress Cataloging-in-Publication Data
Murphy, Stuart J.
    One . . . two . . . three . . . sassafras! / by Stuart J. Murphy ; illustrated by John Wallace.
        p.   cm. — (MathStart)
"Number order."
"Level 1."
Summary: At a family reunion, the cousins line up in order of their ages to get their pictures taken, introducing the concept of numerical order.
ISBN 0-06-028916-3 — ISBN 0-06-028917-1 (lib. bdg.) — ISBN 0-06-446246-3 (pbk.)
1. Sequences (Mathematics)—Juvenile literature.   [1. Sequences (Mathematics)]   I. Wallace, John, ill.   II. Title.   III. Series.
QA246.5.M875   2002   00-054033
515'.24—dc21

Typography by Elynn Cohen   1 2 3 4 5 6 7 8 9 10   ❖   First Edition

One...Two...Three... SASSAFRAS!

Uncle Howie always took the photos at the Lumpkin family reunions. He had a camera that developed the pictures right away.

4

This year he took pictures
of Grandma Zelda dancing
the tango,

Aunt Bertha tasting the
frosting on the cake,

and Uncle Morris's wig
falling into the punch.

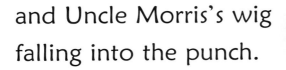

And then it was time for pictures of all the cousins.

"Sally! Max! David!" Uncle Howie yelled. "Come and line up for your picture."

The 3 cousins came running over.

"Where's Bonzo?" Sally said. "We can't take a picture without Bonzo!"

"There's no cousin Bonzo!" said Uncle Howie. But Sally didn't hear.

"Bonzo!" called Sally. "Where are you?"

"Line up from youngest to oldest," said Uncle Howie.

"I'm 6," said Max.

"I'm 9," said Sally.

"I just turned 8," said David. "So I go in between."

Max
6

David
8

Sally
9

"Say, 'Sassafras!'" said Uncle Howie.
"SASSAFRAS!" Max and David yelled.
"Bonzo!" Sally shouted. "There you are!"

And she ran away just before Uncle Howie pressed the button. "Fiddlesticks!" Uncle Howie exclaimed. "The picture's ruined!"

Adam and Briana came to look. "Is it our turn?" asked Briana.

"I'll take all 4 of you together," said Uncle Howie. "Line up from youngest to oldest."

"I'm 11," said Adam. "I'll get over here on the end."

"I'm almost 8," said Briana. "And I want to be next to Adam."

"No way," said David, as he pushed himself between Briana and Adam. "Almost 8 is still only 7."

Max
6

David
8

Briana
7

Adam
11

Max
6

Briana
7

David
8

Adam
11

15

They were finally ready.

"Say, 'Sassafras!'" Uncle Howie said.

"SASSAFRAS!" they all shouted. But just before Uncle Howie pressed the button, Briana poked David, and David bumped into Adam.

"Jumping jelly beans!" exclaimed Uncle Howie. "The picture's ruined!"

Max
6

Briana
7

David
8

Adam
11

Tanya and Leticia walked by with Jacob in his stroller.
"Are you ready for us?" Tanya asked.

"I'll take you all together," said Uncle Howie. "Line up from youngest to oldest."

"I'm 15," said Tanya. She was definitely the oldest.

Max
6

Briana
7

David
8

"I'm 13," said Leticia, "but Adam's a lot taller than me. I'll get between David and him."

Jacob
1

Leticia
13

Adam
11

Tanya
15

"No, no, no!" said Uncle Howie. "Try again!"

"I'm only 11," said Adam to Leticia. "You go between Tanya and me."

"And Jacob belongs down here, next to Max," said Briana.

Jacob
1

Max
6

Briana
7

David
8

Leticia tried to stand on tiptoe so she would
be as tall as Adam.

Adam
11

Leticia
13

Tanya
15

"Say, 'Sassafras!'" said Uncle Howie.

"SASSAFRAS!" everyone shouted.

But just before Uncle Howie pressed the button, Jacob dropped his teddy bear, David poked Briana back, and Leticia couldn't stand on her tiptoes any longer.

"Great galloping gillywhoppers!" Uncle Howie exclaimed. "The picture's ruined!"

"That's it!" said Uncle Howie. "I only have 1 more picture. It has to have everybody in it. Nobody cry. Nobody fall down. And everybody say, 'Sassafras!'"

"Wait! Where's Sally?" Adam asked. "She's the only cousin who's not here!"

"Sally!" everybody yelled.

25

Sally ran over. But she didn't look happy.

"I can't find Bonzo!" she said. "We can't have a family picture without Bonzo!"

"There IS no cousin Bonzo!" Uncle Howie shouted. "Now everybody get in line!"

Jacob
1

Max
6

Briana
7

David
8

"Sally, you're 9, so get between David and me,"
Adam said.

Sally
9

Adam
11

Leticia
13

Tanya
15

"One . . . two . . . three . . . Sassafras!" said Uncle Howie.
"And, Sally, smile!"

Sassafras!

everybody yelled.
Except Sally.

Sally shouted.

Just before Uncle Howie pressed the
button, Bonzo jumped right into Sally's arms.
Uncle Howie was speechless.
"Bonzo!" said Sally. "You're in the picture, too!"

In *One . . . Two . . . Three . . . Sassafras!* the math concept is arranging numbers in order. This concept helps in the development of number sense and enhances counting skills. It also prepares children to understand place value.

If you would like to have more fun with the math concepts presented in *One . . . Two . . . Three . . . Sassafras!* here are a few suggestions:

- Read the story with the child and discuss how Uncle Howie has the children line up by age before he takes a picture.

- There are several ways that the children in the story could have been arranged by Uncle Howie—for example, by height or alphabetically by name. Help the child explore various other possibilities.

- Have the child draw pictures of his or her family. Cut out the drawings and have the child arrange them by age from youngest to oldest.

- Write the numbers 1 through 15 on separate index cards. Mix the cards and remove one from the pile without letting the child see which card you have taken. Then have him or her figure out which card is missing.

- When you count by ones, there is a pattern to the order of the numbers. For example, 3 is one more than 2, and 4 is one more than 3. Discuss this with the child and see if he or she can figure out that each number is always one more than the previous number.

Following are some activities that will help you extend the concepts presented in *One . . . Two . . . Three . . . Sassafras!* into a child's everyday life:

Toy Lineup: Have the child pick 1 toy (for example, 1 teddy bear), then 2 of another toy (for example, 2 dolls), then 5 of another toy (for example, 5 blocks), and so on with whatever numbers you prefer. Then work together to put the piles of toys in order from least to greatest.

Card Game: Take a deck of cards and put aside the tens and the face cards. Each player is dealt 2 cards, which he or she uses to make a 2-digit number. (For example, a player who is dealt an ace and a 9 can make 19 or 91.) The players place their numbers in order. The person with the smallest number collects all the cards. After all the cards have been played, the player with the most cards wins.

Sports: Find the jersey numbers of the players for the child's favorite sports team. These can be found in the newspaper, the team's website, or a program from a game. Have the child place the players in order using the numbers on their jerseys.

The following books include concepts similar to those that are presented in *One . . . Two . . . Three . . . Sassafras!*

- Numbers by Richard L. Allington

- Me First by Helen Lester

- The Robbers Five or Is It Six? by Maria Van Eeden